**Published By Robert Corbin**

@ Omar Noda

Embark on Your Journey to a Flat Stomach:

Achieve Natural Belly Fat Loss Through Lifestyle

Changes

**All Right RESERVED**

ISBN 978-87-94477-15-4

## TABLE OF CONTENTS

Overnight Oats With Fresh Berries And Almonds ............. 1

Quinoa Salad With Roasted Vegetables And Feta ............ 3

Grilled Chicken Salad With Avocado ................................. 5

Cauliflower Fried Rice .......................................................... 7

Grilled Chicken With Sweet Potato Wedges ..................... 9

Spaghetti Squash With Meat Sauce ................................. 11

Tropical Green Smoothie .................................................. 14

Strawberry And Spinach Smoothie .................................. 16

Smoothie With Apples And Broccoli For Detox .............. 18

Smoothie With Figs And Ginger ....................................... 20

Blended Basic Banana ....................................................... 21

Greek Salad With Grilled Shrimp: .................................... 22

Quinoa And Black Bean Salad .......................................... 24

Grilled Salmon With Avocado Salsa ................................ 26

Cherrylemon Juice ............................................................. 28

Bananastrawberry Juice .................................................... 29

Orangecarrot Juice ............................................................ 30

- Proteinpacked Eggs Diablo ............................................. 31
- Calorie Avocadolime Smoothie ....................................... 33
- Maple & Mustard Glazed Ham ........................................ 35
- Smoky Chorizo & Manchego Quiche .............................. 38
- Sautéed Spinach & Homemade Baked Beans ................ 41
- Chicken With Baby Spinach & Tomato Red Wine Sauce 42
- Metabolismboosting Spice Mix ....................................... 45
- Flat Belly Detox Smoothie ............................................... 48
- Slow Cooker Moroccan Chicken With Olives ................. 50
- Chicken Piccata ................................................................ 54
- Slow Cooker African Chicken Stew ................................. 56
- Grilled Salmon With Roasted Vegetables And A Side Salad .................................................................................. 58
- Avocado Toast With Poached Egg And Spinach ............. 61
- Lentil Soup With Mixed Greens ....................................... 63
- Turkey Lettuce Wraps ...................................................... 66
- Baked Lemon Herb Salmon ............................................. 68
- Sushi Rice With A Cucumber Strip .................................. 70

Greek Yogurt ................................................................. 72

Celery Sticks With Peanut Butter ................................... 73

Apple Slices With Almond Butter ................................... 74

Carrot Sticks With Hummus ........................................... 75

Blueberry And Kale Smoothie ........................................ 76

Beet And Carrot Smoothie ............................................. 78

Lowcost Green Smoothie ............................................... 80

Green Chocolate Smoothie ............................................ 81

Green Smoothie With A Twist ........................................ 83

Quinoa And Vegetable Stirfry......................................... 85

Grilled Chicken With Sweet Potato Wedges .................. 87

Grilled Chicken Salad...................................................... 89

Papayalime Juice ............................................................ 91

Cranberryapple Juice...................................................... 92

Lemonblueberry Juice .................................................... 93

Acaiblueberry Smoothie Bowl........................................ 95

Egginahole With Spinach & Bacon ................................. 97

Parmesan Cloud Eggs ................................................... 100

Raised Pork Pie ................................................................. 102

Ginger Chicken & Green Bean Noodles ......................... 106

Teriyaki Salmon With Grilled Zucchini .......................... 108

Savory Brown Rice With Vegetables .............................. 110

Shrimp And Brown Rice Risotto ..................................... 112

Blueberry Basil Weight Loss Smoothie .......................... 114

Cabbage Fatburning Soup ............................................. 116

Drink With Mango & Basil .............................................. 118

Chicken Piccata .............................................................. 120

Slow Cooker African Chicken Stew ................................ 122

Greek Yogurt With Chia Seeds ....................................... 124

Hummus And Veggies .................................................... 126

Baked Sweet Potato With Black Beans And Salad ........ 128

Grilled Chicken With Zucchini Noodles ......................... 131

Roasted Chickpeas ......................................................... 136

Creamy Green Smoothie ................................................ 138

Pineapple And Kale Smoothie ........................................ 140

Mango And Celery Smoothie ......................................... 142

Fruity Green Smoothie .................................................. 143

**Overnight Oats With Fresh Berries And Almonds**

**Ingredients:**

- 1/4 cup fresh berries (strawberries, raspberries, blueberries, etc.)
- 1/4 cup sliced almonds
- 1 tablespoon honey (or another sweetener)
- 1/4 teaspoon cinnamon
- 1/2 cup rolled oats
- 1/2 cup almond milk
- 1/4 cup plain yogurt

**Directions:**

1. In a bowl, mix the oats, almond milk, yogurt, honey, and cinnamon until well combined.

2. Place the mixture in a mason jar or other airtight container and refrigerate overnight.
3. In the morning, top the oats with fresh berries and almonds. Enjoy!

**Quinoa Salad With Roasted Vegetables And Feta**

**Ingredients:**

- 2 tablespoons olive oil

- 2 tablespoons white balsamic vinegar

- 1 teaspoon honey

- Salt and pepper to taste

- 2 cups cooked quinoa

- 2 cups diced roasted vegetables, such as red peppers, zucchini, squash, carrots, etc.

- 1/2 cup crumbled feta

- 2 tablespoons chopped fresh herbs, such as parsley, mint, or basil

**Directions:**

1. Set the oven to 400 degrees Fahrenheit.

2. Line a baking sheet with parchment paper and spread the diced vegetables on the sheet. Sprinkle with salt and pepper then drizzle with olive oil. Vegetables should be roasted for 1520 minutes, or until they are soft and lightly browned.3.
3. In a large bowl, combine the cooked quinoa, roasted vegetables, and feta.
4. In a small bowl, whisk together the olive oil, white balsamic vinegar, honey, and salt and pepper.
5. Pour the dressing over the quinoa mixture and toss to combine.
6. Sprinkle the chopped herbs over the top and serve. Enjoy!

## Grilled Chicken Salad With Avocado

**Ingredients:**

- Cucumber, sliced
- Red onion, thinly sliced
- Avocado, diced
- Lemon juice
- Extra virgin olive oil
- 4 ounces grilled chicken breast, sliced
- Mixed salad greens
- Cherry tomatoes, halved
- Salt and pepper to taste

**Directions:**

1. In a bowl, combine the mixed salad greens, cherry tomatoes, cucumber, red onion, and diced avocado.
2. Squeeze lemon juice over the salad for a refreshing flavor.
3. Sprinkle extra virgin olive oil and season with salt and pepper.
4. Add the sliced grilled chicken on top.
5. Toss everything gently to combine and enjoy a nutrientrich and satisfying salad.

## Cauliflower Fried Rice

**Ingredients:**

- 1 small head of cauliflower, grated or riced 4 ounces cooked shrimp or chicken, diced

- Assorted vegetables (e.g., peas, carrots, bell peppers), diced

- 2 cloves garlic, minced

- 2 tablespoons lowsodium soy sauce or tamari

- 1 tablespoon sesame oil

- 2 green onions, sliced

- Optional addins: scrambled egg, chopped cashews, sesame seeds

**Directions:**

1. In a large skillet, heat sesame oil over low heat.
2. Add minced garlic and cook for 1 minute until it becomes fragrant.
3. Add the diced vegetables and stirfry for 34
4. minutes until they are tendercrisp.
5. Add the grated or riced cauliflower to the skillet and stirfry for another 2 minutes.
6. Stir in the cooked shrimp or chicken and continue to cook for 23 minutes.
7. Pour in soy sauce or tamari and toss everything together.
8. If desired, push the cauliflower mixture to one side of the skillet and scramble an egg on the other side.
9. Once the egg is cooked, mix it into the cauliflower mixture.
10. Remove from heat and garnish with sliced green onions, chopped cashews, or sesame seeds if desired.

## Grilled Chicken With Sweet Potato Wedges

**Ingredients:**

- 3 tbsp olive oil
- 1 tsp paprika
- 1 tsp garlic powder
- 4 boneless, skinless chicken breasts
- 2 large sweet potatoes, peeled and cut into wedges
- Salt and pepper to taste

**Directions:**

1. Preheat the grill to mediumhigh heat.
2. In a small bowl, combine the olive oil, paprika, garlic powder, salt, and pepper.
3. Brush the chicken breasts and sweet potato wedges with the olive oil mixture.

4. Place the chicken breasts on the grill and cook for 68 minutes on each side, or until the chicken is cooked through.
5. Place the sweet potato wedges on the grill and cook for 1012 minutes, or until tender and lightly browned.
6. Serve the grilled chicken with the sweet potato wedges.

## Spaghetti Squash With Meat Sauce

**Ingredients:**

- 2 garlic cloves, minced
- 1 can (28 oz) crushed tomatoes
- 1 tsp dried oregano
- 1 tsp dried basil
- Salt and pepper to taste
- 1 medium spaghetti squash
- 1 lb ground beef
- 1 onion, diced
- Optional: grated Parmesan cheese for topping

**Directions:**

1. Preheat the oven to 400°F (200°C). Cut the spaghetti squash in half lengthwise and scoop out the seeds.
2. Place the spaghetti squash halves on a baking sheet, cutside down, and bake for 3540 minutes, or until the squash is tender.
3. While the spaghetti squash is baking, heat a large skillet over mediumhigh heat.
4. Add the ground beef to the skillet and cook for 57 minutes, or until browned.
5. Add the diced onion and minced garlic to the skillet and cook for an additional 23 minutes, or until softened.
6. Add the crushed tomatoes, oregano, and basil to the skillet and stir to combine.
7. Reduce the heat to low and let the sauce simmer for 1015 minutes, or until it has thickened.
8. Season the meat sauce with salt and pepper to taste.

9. Once the spaghetti squash is done baking, use a fork to scrape the flesh of the squash into strands.
10. Serve the spaghetti squash topped with the meat sauce and grated Parmesan cheese, if desired.

**Tropical Green Smoothie**

**Ingredients:**

- 1 cup fresh spinach leaves
- 1/2 cup unsweetened coconut milk
- 1/2 cup water
- 1 tablespoon honey
- 1 tablespoon chia seeds
- 1/2 cup chopped pineapple
- 1/2 cup chopped mango
- 1 banana
- Ice cubes (optional)

**Directions:**

1. Begin by washing all the fresh produce thoroughly.
2. Add the pineapple, mango, banana, spinach, coconut milk, water, and honey to a blender.
3. Blend on high speed for about 12 minutes, or until the mixture is smooth and creamy.
4. If you like your smoothie colder, add a few ice cubes and blend again.
5. Finally, add the chia seeds and blend briefly until they are evenly distributed throughout the smoothie.
6. Pour the smoothie into a tall glass and enjoy!

## Strawberry And Spinach Smoothie

**Ingredients:**

- 1/2 cup unsweetened almond milk
- 1/2 cup water
- 1/2 banana
- 1 tablespoon honey (optional)
- 1 cup frozen strawberries
- 1 cup fresh spinach leaves
- Ice cubes (optional)

**Directions:**

1. Begin by washing all the fresh produce thoroughly.

2. Add the frozen strawberries, fresh spinach, almond milk, water, banana, and honey (if using) to a blender.
3. Blend on high speed for about 12 minutes, or until the mixture is smooth and crcreamy
4. If you like your smoothie colder, add a few ice cubes and blend again.
5. Pour the smoothie into a tall glass and enjoy!

# Smoothie With Apples And Broccoli For Detox

**Ingredients:**

- ½ orange
- ½ cup pure water
- 1 cup cubed ice
- 1 cup romaine lettuce, shredded
- ½ cup broccoli stems
- 1 apple, medium size

**Directions:**

1. Clean the greens well under running water.
2. Core and peel the apple. Make 1inch cubes.
3. Peel the orange. Remove the seeds and cut them into pieces.

4. Put all items in a blender. Mix on high until completely incorporated.
5. Strain into a glass and serve.

# Smoothie With Figs And Ginger

**Ingredients:**

- 2 pitted dates in their entirety (presoaked)
- ½ cup of water
- 1 cup cubed ice
- 1 pound spinach
- 1 cup dried figs (about 4 mediumsized fruits)
- ½ tbsp minced ginger

**Directions:**

1. Combine spinach and water in a blender. Mix until completely smooth.
2. Add the other Ingredients: and process until smooth.
3. Strain into a glass and serve.

## Blended Basic Banana

**Ingredients:**

- ½ cup pure water
- ½ cup ice cubes.
- 1 cup kale leaves, chopped
- 2 cups of ripe bananas, chopped

**Directions:**

1. Thoroughly clean the kale with running water.
2. Peel and cut bananas into 1inch pieces.
3. In a blender, combine all Ingredients: and mix until smooth.
4. Strain into a glass and serve.

## Greek Salad With Grilled Shrimp:

**Ingredients:**

- 1 red bell pepper, chopped
- 1/2 red onion, sliced
- 1/2 cup kalamata olives
- 1/2 cup crumbled feta cheese
- Juice of 1 lemon
- 2 tablespoons red wine vinegar
- 1 pound large shrimp, peeled and deveined
- 2 tablespoons olive oil
- 2 teaspoons dried oregano
- Salt and pepper to taste
- 1 head romaine lettuce, chopped

- 1 cucumber, chopped

- 1 clove of garlic, minced

**Directions:**

1. Preheat the grill to medium heat.
2. In a small bowl, mix together the olive oil, oregano, salt, and pepper. Toss the shrimp in the mixture.
3. Grill the shrimp for 23 minutes on each side, or until pink and cooked through.
4. In a large bowl, combine the lettuce, cucumber, bell pepper, onion, olives, and feta cheese.
5. In a small bowl, whisk together the lemon juice, red wine vinegar, garlic, salt, and pepper. Drizzle the dressing over the salad.
6. Serve the grilled shrimp on top of the salad.

## Quinoa And Black Bean Salad

**Ingredients:**

- 1/2 red onion, chopped
- 1/2 cup corn kernels
- 1/4 cup chopped fresh cilantro
- Juice of 1 lime
- 2 tablespoons olive oil
- 1 cup quinoa, cooked
- 1 can black beans, drained and rinsed
- 1 red bell pepper, chopped
- Salt and pepper to taste

**Directions:**

1. In a large bowl, combine the cooked quinoa, black beans, bell pepper, onion, corn, and cilantro.
2. In a small bowl, whisk together the lime juice, olive oil, salt, and pepper. Drizzle the dressing over the salad and toss to coat.
3. Chill the salad in the refrigerator for at least 30 minutes before serving.

# Grilled Salmon With Avocado Salsa

**Ingredients:**

- 1 small jalapeno pepper, seeded and finely diced
- 1/4 cup chopped fresh cilantro
- 2 tbsp fresh lime juice
- Salt and pepper
- 4 6ounce salmon fillets
- 2 ripe avocados, peeled and diced
- 1/2 red onion, finely diced
- Olive oil

**Directions:**

1. Preheat grill to mediumhigh heat.

2. Brush salmon fillets with olive oil and season with salt and pepper.
3. Grill salmon for 45 minutes per side or until cooked through.
4. In a bowl, mix together avocado, red onion, jalapeno pepper, cilantro, lime juice, salt, and pepper.
5. Serve grilled salmon topped with avocado salsa.

# Cherrylemon Juice

**Ingredients:**

- 100g of fresh cherries
- 1 lemon (juiced)
- 240ml of water
- 1 tablespoon of honey or maple syrup (optional)

**Directions:**

1. Remove the pits from the cherry.
2. Quarter the lemon.
3. Juice the cherries, lemon juice and water together using a juicer.
4. To get rid of any pulp, filter the juice through a finemesh screen.
5. Add honey or maple syrup if desired
6. Juice should be served cold or over ice.

## Bananastrawberry Juice

**Ingredients:**

- 240ml of almond milk (or any preferred milk)
- 1 tablespoon of honey (optional)
- 150g of bananas
- 150g of fresh strawberries

**Directions:**

1. Bananas and strawberries should all be cut into tiny pieces.
2. Juice the Ingredients: together with almond milk until smooth.
3. Add a little water if you desire a thinner consistency.
4. If a sweeter drink is desired, add a tablespoon of honey.
5. Serve immediately.

## Orangecarrot Juice

**Ingredients:**

- 300g of carrots
- 200g of oranges
- 120ml of water

**Directions:**

1. Oranges and carrots should be well washed.
2. Peel the oranges, then chop the carrots into tiny pieces.
3. Juice the peeled oranges, chopped carrots and water in a juicer until smooth.
4. Serve the juice immediately by pouring it into a glass.

## Proteinpacked Eggs Diablo

**Ingredients:**

- 1 8oz can nosaltadded tomato sauce
- ½ tsp crushed red pepper flakes
- 8 eggs
- 2 Tbsp sliced green onions (scallions)
- 8 corn tortillas, warmed
- 1 Tbsp olive oil
- 1 medium onion, chopped
- 1 medium green bell pepper, chopped
- 1 Tbsp minced garlic
- 1 14.5oz can nosaltadded fireroasted diced tomatoes, undrained

- Salt and black pepper to taste

**Directions:**

1. In a large skillet, heat oil over medium heat. Add the chopped onion, pepper, and garlic.
2. Cook for 3 to 4 minutes, stirring occasionally until vegetables are tender.
3. Add tomatoes, tomato sauce, and red pepper flakes. Cook for 5 minutes, or until sauce is bubbling around edges.
4. Form a small indentation in the sauce. Break an egg into a cup and slip into sauce; repeat with remaining eggs.
5. Cover pan and cook 3 to 5 minutes, or until egg whites are completely set and yolks start to thicken.
6. Sprinkle eggs with green onions. Serve with corn tortillas. Season with salt and pepper.

## Calorie Avocadolime Smoothie

**Ingredients:**

- 1/3 cup chopped peeled pear
- ¼ mediumsize ripe avocado, seeded and peeled
- 2 Tbsp. honey
- ¼ tsp. lime zest
- 1 Tbsp. lime juice
- 1 cup ice
- ½ cup light coconut milk
- 1/3 cup chopped celery
- Fresh mint and/or lime slice

**Directions:**

1. In a blender, combine ice, coconut milk, celery, pear, avocado, honey, lime zest, and lime juice.
2. Cover and blend about 1 minute or until smooth. Garnish with mint or a lime slice.

## Maple & Mustard Glazed Ham

**Ingredients:**

- about 25 whole cloves
- For the glaze
- 200ml maple syrup
- 2 tbsp coarsegrain mustard
- 2 tbsp Worcestershire sauce
- 2 tbsp soy sauce
- 1 whole leg of gammon, smoked or unsmoked, around 5kg weight bonein
- 1 cinnamon stick
- 1 tsp peppercorns
- 1 tsp coriander seeds

- 2 bay leaves

**Directions:**

1. Put the gammon in a very large pan and cover with cold water. Add the spices and bay.
2. Bring to the boil, then turn down and simmer for around 1 hr 50 mins, topping up the water level with boiling water, if necessary. Scoop off any scum that rises to the top every now and then.
3. Carefully pour the liquid away (I like to keep it for making soup), then let the ham cool a little while you heat the oven to 190C/fan 170C/gas 5.
4. Lift the ham into a large roasting tin, then cut away the skin leaving behind an even layer of fat.
5. Score the fat all over in a crisscross pattern, then stud cloves all over the ham.
6. Can now be chilled for up to 2 days.

7. Mix the glaze **Ingredients:**in a jug. Pour half over the fat, roast for 15 mins, then pour over the rest and return to the oven for another 35 mins, basting with the pan juices 34 times as it bakes. Turn the pan around a few times during cooking so the fat colours evenly. Remove from the oven and allow to rest for 15 mins before carving.
8. Can be roasted on the day or up to 2 days ahead and served cold.

## Smoky Chorizo & Manchego Quiche

**Ingredients:**

- 150g manchego cheese, grated
- For the pastry
- 250g plain flour, plus extra for dusting
- 1½ tbsp smoked paprika
- ½ tsp cayenne pepper
- 1 tbsp olive oil
- 200g chorizo ring, cut into small cubes
- 3 large eggs
- 100g crème fraîche, plus extra to serve
- 150g double cream
- 100g cold unsalted butter, cubed

**Directions:**

1. Heat the oil in a medium frying pan over a high heat, and fry the chorizo for 45 mins until crisp.
2. Transfer to a plate lined with kitchen paper using a slotted spoon, and set aside to cool. Set the pan with the fat aside, and leave to cool.
3. For the pastry, put the flour, 1/2 tsp salt, the paprika, cayenne pepper, cooled chorizo fat and the butter in the bowl of a large food processor and blitz until the mixture looks like coarse breadcrumbs.
4. Gradually pulse in 4 tbsp cold water until it comes together into a dough.
5. Turn out onto a lightly floured surface, and knead gently until smooth. Wrap the dough and chill for at least 10 mins. Will keep chilled for up to three days.

6. Heat the oven to 200C/180C fan/gas 6. Roll the chilled pastry out on a floured work surface to the thickness of a 50p coin then lift it into a 23cm loosebottomed tart tin, leaving an overhang.
7. Prick the base all over with a fork, line with baking parchment, then fill with baking beans. Transfer to a baking sheet and bake for 15 mins.
8. Remove the parchment and beans, then bake for 1520 mins more until golden and crisp. Trim away the pastry that is overhanging using a serrated knife.
9. Meanwhile, whisk the eggs, crème fraîche and cream together, season, then stir in the cheese and cooled chorizo.
10. Pour into the pastry case and bake for 2530 mins until the filling is just set. Leave to cool in the tin, then remove from the tin and slice. Will keep in the fridge for up to three days.

## Sautéed Spinach & Homemade Baked Beans

**Ingredients:**

- 2 tbsp. walnuts, chopped
- 1 tsp. garlic, minced
- 3 tbsp. lemon juice
- 1 lb. baby spinach leaves
- 1 tbsp. extravirgin olive oil

**Directions:**

1. Cook the spinach in a pot of boiling water until just wilting, remove and drain well.
2. Add olive oil to a hot skillet and sauté garlic until it is browned, add walnuts sauté a little longer, then add the spinach and sauté for 3 further minutes.

3. Transfer to 2 warm plates and drizzle lemon juice over each. Enjoy!

## Chicken With Baby Spinach & Tomato Red Wine Sauce

**Ingredients:**

- 2 tbsp red wine vinegar

- 1/3 cup lowsodium chicken broth (preferably home made)

- 10 grape tomatoes, chopped with juice

- 2 cups of brown rice, cooked

- 1 tbsp extra virgin olive oil

- 3 garlic cloves, peeled, chopped

- 2 (8oz.) chicken breasts, halved, boneless, skinless

- 8oz. of baby spinach, washed

**Directions:**

1. Heat a large pan over a medium to high heat. Add the virgin olive oil.
2. When heated add the chopped garlic and cook for a minute or so.
3. Add the chicken breasts and cook each side until browned and juices are running clear.
4. Remove the cooked chicken breasts and set them aside.
5. Add to the same pan the baby spinach and cook until wilting.
6. Remove the baby spinach from the pan and set it aside.
7. Then lower the heat to medium and pour in the red wine vinegar then the chicken broth as well and stir, collecting the browned bits in the bottom of the pan to add more flavor.

8. Then add the chopped grape tomatoes, bring the sauce to a simmer and cook 3 or 4 minutes.
9. Place the rice in a large serving bowl. Top the brown rice with the baby spinach, half chicken breasts and red wine tomato sauce. Serve

# Metabolismboosting Spice Mix

**INGREDIENTS:**

**SEEDS**

- 2 tsp ajwain (seeds)
- 1 tbsp kalonji (seeds)
- 1 tsp cardamom (seeds)
- 1 tsp black peppercorns
- 3 tbsp coriander (seeds)
- 2 tbsp cumin (seeds)
- 1 tbsp fenugreek (seeds)

**POWDERS**

- 2 tsp ginger (powder)

- 2 tsp turmeric (powder)

- 1 tsp Ceylon cinnamon (powder)

**DIRECTIONS:**

**RAW:**

1. Mix all ingredients in the bowl, transfer the mixture into the electric grinder or spice mill and grind to a fine powder.
2. Store in an airtight jar in a dark place

**DRY ROAST**

3. Using a skillet, dry toast the spices. Fenugreek and cardmom can be roasted in the same pan. Ajwain and kalonji can also be roasted together.
4. Coriander and cumin must be roasted in separate pans. Roast all on mediumlow heat until fragrant, but don't let them brown.
5. Transfer spices into a bowl immediately because even if you turn off the heat, they

will continue cooking on a hot pan and might burn. While seeds are still hot, mix in cinnamon, ginger, and turmeric powders. Set aside to cool a bit.
6. Grind to a fine powder using a coffee grinder
7. Place in an airtight spice jar and store in a cool, dark, dry place

## Flat Belly Detox Smoothie

**INGREDIENTS:**

- 1 tsp cinnamon
- 1 cup mixed berries
- 1/4 avocado
- 1/2 cup yogurt
- 1/2 cup spinach
- 1 frozen banana
- 1/4 cup oats
- 1 cup oat milk

**DIRECTIONS:**

1. Add greens and oats to blender with oat milk and blend.

2. Add rest of ingredients and blend on high speed until smooth.
3. Enjoy!

## Slow Cooker Moroccan Chicken With Olives

**Ingredients:**

**Chicken**

- 1 carrot, sliced

- 1 large onion

- 30 small black olives, pitted (about 1 cup)

- 3 cloves garlic, minced

- 2 pounds boneless, skinless chicken breast halves

- 1/2 cup chopped fresh cilantro (optional)

- 1/2 cup reducedsodium chicken broth

- 1/4 cup allpurpose flour

- 3 Tbsp olive oil

- 2 tsp ground cumin
- 1/2 tsp freshly ground black pepper
- 1/4 tsp salt
- 1 can (14½ ounces) nosaltadded stewed tomatoes

**Harissa**

- 1 tsp ground caraway seed
- 1/4 tsp salt
- 3 Tbsp olive oil
- 3/4 cup dried hot red chile peppers, such as guajillo
- 2 cloves garlic, minced
- 1 tsp ground coriander

**Directions:**

1. PREPARE the chicken: Coat the stoneware of a slow cooker pot with cooking spray. Combine the broth, flour, oil, cumin, pepper, and salt in the pot. Whisk until smooth.
2. Add the tomatoes (with juice), carrot, onion, olives, and garlic. Stir to mix. Tuck the chicken into the pot, covering with the other ingredients.
3. Cover and cook on low for 5 to 6 hours or on high for 3 to 4 hours.
4. PREPARE the harissa: Remove the stems and seeds from the peppers and discard. Soak the peppers in warm water for about 1 hour or until softened.
5. Drain and transfer to a food processor fitted with a metal blade or a blender.
6. Add the garlic, coriander, caraway seed, and salt. Process, scraping the sides of the bowl as needed, until a paste forms. Drizzle in the oil

through the tube to reach a smooth consistency.
7. STIR in the cilantro (if using) just before serving. Pass the harissa at the table.

## Chicken Piccata

**Ingredients:**

- 2 Tbsp chopped fresh parsley
- 2 tsp capers, minced
- Freshly ground black pepper
- 12 ounces boneless, skinless chicken tenders
- 2 Tbsp flour
- 4 Tbsp olive oil
- 2 freshly squeezed lemon juice

**Directions:**

1. LAY the tenders on a work surface. With a smooth scaloppine pounder or a rolling pin covered in plastic wrap, flatten to 1/4"

thickness. Dredge the cutlets lightly in the flour.

2. HEAT a large skillet over mediumhigh heat. Add the oil to the skillet and heat until sizzling. Place the chicken in the skillet. Cook for 2 minutes per side or until lightly browned and cooked through.

3. ADD the lemon juice, parsley, and capers. Bring the mixture to a boil. Reduce the heat and simmer for 2 minutes to allow the flavors to blend. Season to taste with the pepper. Serve the chicken with the pan juices.

## Slow Cooker African Chicken Stew

**Ingredients:**

- 1 sweet potato, peeled and cubed
- 1 can (14½ ounces) reducedsodium chicken broth
- 1/2 cup chunky natural unsalted peanut butter
- 2 Tbsp tomato paste
- 1/4 tsp salt
- 1 Tbsp peanut oil
- 12 ounces boneless, skinless chicken thighs, trimmed and cut into 24 pieces
- 1 onion, chopped
- 3 cloves garlic, minced

- 1 jalapeno chile pepper, seeded and chopped

- 1 carrot, thickly sliced

- 1/4 tsp freshly ground black pepper

**Directions:**

1. HEAT the oil in a large nonstick skillet over mediumhigh heat. Add the chicken and cook, stirring occasionally, for 3 to 4 minutes or until lightly browned.
2. Transfer to a 4quart slow cooker. Return the skillet to the heat and add the onion, garlic, chile pepper, and carrot.
3. Cook for 1 minute, then transfer to the slow cooker. Stir in the sweet potato, broth, peanut butter, and tomato paste.
4. COOK on high for 3 to 4 hours or low for 5 to 6 hours or until the chicken and vegetables are very tender. Season with salt and black pepper.

## Grilled Salmon With Roasted Vegetables And A Side Salad

**Ingredients:**

- 4 (4ounce) salmon fillets
- 2 tablespoons olive oil
- Salt and pepper to taste
- 2 red bell peppers, cut into strips
- 2 yellow bell peppers, cut into strips
- 2 zucchinis, cut into thin slices
- 2 tablespoons minced garlic
- 1 tablespoon oregano
- 1 tablespoon thyme
- 1 tablespoon rosemary

- 1 tablespoon lemon juice

**For the side salad:**

- 1 head romaine lettuce, chopped
- 1/2 cucumber, chopped
- 1/2 red onion, thinly sliced
- 1/2 cup cherry tomatoes, halved
- 1/4 cup crumbled feta cheese
- 1 tablespoon olive oil
- 1 tablespoon balsamic vinegar
- Salt and pepper to taste

**Directions:**

1. Preheat the grill to mediumhigh heat.
2. Brush the salmon fillets with olive oil and season with salt and pepper.

3. Place the salmon fillets on the preheated grill. Flip once halfway through cooking for roughly 8 minutes.
4. Meanwhile, in a large bowl, combine the bell peppers, zucchini, garlic, oregano, thyme, rosemary, and lemon juice.
1. Add a little olive oil and mix everything.
5. Place the vegetables on the preheated grill. Cook for about 10 minutes, stirring occasionally until the vegetables are slightly charred and tender.
6. For the side salad, combine the lettuce, cucumber, red onion, cherry tomatoes, feta cheese, olive oil, balsamic vinegar, salt, and pepper in a large bowl. Toss to combine.
7. Serve the grilled salmon with roasted vegetables and a side salad. Enjoy!

## Avocado Toast With Poached Egg And Spinach

**Ingredients:**

- 1/2 cup of spinach

- 2 eggs

- 1 tablespoon of olive oil

- 2 slices of bread

- 1/2 avocado

- Salt and pepper to taste

**Directions:**

1. Preheat your oven to 350 degrees.
2. Lightly toast the bread slices to a golden color.
3. Mash the avocado with a fork and spread it on the toasted bread slices.

4. Heat the olive oil in a skillet on average heat. After adding, cook the spinach for 2–3 minutes, or until wilted.
5. Meanwhile, bring a pot of water to a boil and poach the eggs for 34 minutes until the whites are cooked through.
6. Place the poached eggs on top of the avocado toast and top with the sautéed spinach.
7. Use your discretion when adding salt and pepper. Enjoy!

**Lentil Soup With Mixed Greens**

**Ingredients:**

- 1 teaspoon ground coriander

- 1/2 teaspoon smoked paprika

- 1/2 teaspoon turmeric

- 1/2 teaspoon ground black pepper

- 6 cups vegetable broth

- 2 cups mixed greens (such as kale, spinach, chard, and/or collards)

- 1/4 cup fresh lemon juice

- 1 cup of dry lentils

- 2 tablespoons olive oil

- 1 medium onion, diced

- 2 cloves of garlic, minced

- 1 teaspoon ground cumin

- 1/4 cup freshly chopped parsley

**Directions:**

1. Rinse the lentils in a mesh strainer and set aside.
2. Heat the olive oil in a large pot over mediumhigh heat.
3. Add the onion and garlic and cook, stirring often, until the onion is softened and lightly browned, about 5 minutes.
4. Add the cumin, coriander, smoked paprika, turmeric, and black pepper and cook, stirring, for 1 minute.
5. Add the vegetable broth and lentils, bring to a boil, reduce the heat to low, and simmer, covered, for 30 minutes.

6. Add the mixed greens and cook for an additional 10 minutes.
7. Stir in the lemon juice and parsley and season with salt and pepper.
8. Serve warm. Enjoy!

## Turkey Lettuce Wraps

**Ingredients:**

- 810 large lettuce leaves

- 1 pound ground turkey

- 1 tablespoon olive oil

- 2 cloves garlic, minced

- 1 tablespoon grated ginger

- 2 tablespoons lowsodium soy sauce or tamari
  1 tablespoon hoisin sauce

- Sliced bell peppers

- Shredded carrots

- Sliced green onions

- Sesame seeds (optional)

**Directions:**

1. Heat olive oil in a large skillet over low heat.
2. Add minced garlic and grated ginger to the skillet and cook for about 1 minute until fragrant.
3. Add ground turkey to the skillet and cook until browned and cooked through, breaking it up with a spatula.
4. In a small bowl, whisk together soy sauce or tamari and hoisin sauce.
5. Pour the sauce over the cooked ground turkey and stir to coat evenly.
6. Add sliced bell peppers, shredded carrots, and sliced green onions to the skillet.
7. Cook for an additional 23 minutes until the vegetables are tendercrisp.
8. Remove from heat and sprinkle with sesame seeds if desired.

9. Spoon the turkey mixture onto the lettuce leaves, wrap them up, and enjoy these flavorful and lowcarb turkey lettuce wraps.

### Baked Lemon Herb Salmon

**Ingredients:**

- 1 tablespoon olive oil
- 2 cloves garlic, minced
- 1 teaspoon dried dill
- 1 teaspoon dried thyme
- 2 salmon fillets
- Juice of 1 lemon
- Salt and pepper to taste

**Directions:**

1. Preheat the oven to 400°F (200°C) and using a parchment paper line a baking sheet
2. Place the salmon fillets on the already prepared baking sheet.
3. In a small bowl, whisk together lemon juice, olive oil, minced garlic, dried dill, dried thyme, salt, and pepper.
4. Pour the lemon herb mixture over the salmon fillets, making sure they are well coated.
5. Bake in the preheated oven for about 1215 minutes until the salmon is well cooked and flakes easily with a fork.

## Sushi Rice With A Cucumber Strip

**Ingredients:**

- Drained tuna  1 can
- Diced thin strips of cucumber  1
- Nori  34 sheets
- Cooked sushi rice  1 cup
- Vinegar  1 tablespoon
- Sugar  1 teaspoon
- Salt  1 teaspoon

**Directions:**

1. Mix the sugar, salt, and vinegar with the sushi rice. Have it cooked according to the instructions.

2. On a bamboo rolling mat, place a sheet of nori and spread the sushi rice evenly
3. Place the tuna and cucumber strips in a line on one end of the nori.
4. Using the bamboo rolling mat, form a log by rolling up the nori and sushi rice.
5. With a sharp edge knife, slice the rolled nori and sushi rice into about 8 pieces.
6. Sprinkle with sesame seeds if desired and enjoy.

## Greek Yogurt

**Ingredients:**

- Greek yogurt  1 cup
- Honey  1 tablespoon
- Ice cubes  45 (optional)

**Directions:**

1. In a bowl, combine the Greek yogurt and honey.
2. Mix until it is well blended.
3. Add the ice cubes to chill (optional)

## Celery Sticks With Peanut Butter

**Ingredients:**

- 46 celery sticks
- 23 tablespoons natural peanut butter

**Directions:**

1. Wash the celery sticks and cut them into 34 inch pieces.
2. Spread peanut butter onto one end of each celery stick.
3. Serve and enjoy as a healthy snack!

## Apple Slices With Almond Butter

**Ingredients:**

- 1 apple, cored and sliced
- 23 tablespoons natural almond butter

**Directions:**

1. Wash the apple and cut it into thin slices.
2. Spread almond butter onto one side of each apple slice.
3. Serve and enjoy as a healthy snack!

## Carrot Sticks With Hummus

**Ingredients:**

- 46 mediumsized carrots, peeled and cut into sticks
- 1/2 cup hummus

**Directions:**

1. Wash the carrots and peel them. Cut them into sticks.
2. Place the hummus in a bowl.
3. Arrange the carrot sticks around the hummus bowl.
4. Serve and enjoy as a healthy snack!

# Blueberry And Kale Smoothie

**Ingredients:**

- 1/2 banana
- 1/2 cup unsweetened almond milk
- 1/2 cup water
- 1 tablespoon chia seeds
- 1 cup fresh kale, chopped
- 1/2 cup frozen blueberries
- Ice cubes (optional)

**Directions:**

1. Begin by washing all the fresh produce thoroughly.
2. Add the fresh kale, frozen blueberries, banana, almond milk, water, and chia seeds to a blender.

3. Blend on high speed for about 12 minutes, or until the mixture is smooth and creamy.
4. If you like your smoothie colder, add a few ice cubes and blend again.
5. Pour the smoothie into a tall glass and enjoy!

## Beet And Carrot Smoothie

**Ingredients:**

- 1/2 cup Greek yogurt
- 1 tablespoon honey
- 1 tablespoon flax seeds (optional)
- 1/2 teaspoon ground ginger
- 1/2 teaspoon ground cinnamon
- 1 mediumsized beetroot
- 2 mediumsized carrots
- 1 small banana
- 1/2 cup unsweetened almond milk
- 1/2 cup ice cubes

**Directions:**

1. Peel and chop the beetroot and carrots into small pieces.
2. In a blender, add the chopped beetroot and carrots, banana, almond milk, Greek yogurt, honey, flax seeds, ground ginger, and ground cinnamon.
3. Blend all the Ingredients: until smooth.
4. Add the ice cubes and blend again until the mixture is creamy and smooth.
5. Pour the smoothie into two glasses and serve immediately.

## Lowcost Green Smoothie

**Ingredients:**

- ½ cucumber slices
- 1 cup of water
- 2 apple slices
- 1 pound banana

**Directions:**

1. Apples should be peeled, cored, and cut into 1inch cubes.
2. Peel and cut the banana into 1inch pieces.
3. Cut cucumbers into 1inch cubes without peeling.
4. In a blender, combine all Ingredients: and mix until smooth.
5. Pour into a glass and serve right away.

## Green Chocolate Smoothie

**Ingredients:**

- 1 cup bananas, sliced
- 1 teaspoon cacao powder,
- Unsweetened 1 tbsp. natural honey
- 1 cup coconut water, unsweetened
- ½ cup finely chopped kale leaves
- 1 cup romaine lettuce leaves, chopped
- ½ cup of Swiss chard

**Directions:**

1. Clean and prepare the greens and fruits.
2. Peel and cut bananas into 1inch pieces.
3. In a blender, combine all Ingredients: and pulse until smooth.

4. Pour into a glass and serve right away.

## Green Smoothie With A Twist

**Ingredients:**

- ½ avocados

- 1 green apple, medium size

- ½ cup purified water

- ½ cup cubed ice

- 1 cup of kale leaves, chopped

- 1 pound Brussels sprouts

- ½ cup fresh spinach leaves

**Directions:**

1. Prepare the greens by washing and preparing them.
2. Remove the avocado flesh. Remove the seed.

3. Core the apple and cut it into 1inch pieces without peeling.
4. Puree the kale, Brussels sprouts, spinach, and filtered water in a blender until smooth.
5. Stir in the avocado, apple, and ice cubes. Mix until completely smooth.

## Quinoa And Vegetable Stirfry

**Ingredients:**

- 1 yellow squash, sliced
- 1 onion, sliced
- 2 cloves garlic, minced
- 1 tsp grated ginger
- 2 tbsp lowsodium soy sauce
- 1 cup quinoa, rinsed and drained
- 2 cups vegetable broth
- 1 tbsp olive oil
- 1 red bell pepper, sliced
- 1 yellow bell pepper, sliced

- 1 zucchini, sliced

- 2 tbsp chopped fresh cilantro

**Directions:**

1. In a medium saucepan, combine quinoa and vegetable broth. Bring to a boil, then reduce heat and simmer for 15-20 minutes or until quinoa is tender and liquid is absorbed.
2. In a large skillet, heat olive oil over medium-high heat. Add bell peppers, zucchini, yellow squash, onion, garlic, and ginger. Stir-fry for 5-7 minutes or until vegetables are tender.
3. Add cooked quinoa to the skillet and stir-fry for another 2-3 minutes.
4. Stir in soy sauce and cilantro.
5. Serve hot.

## Grilled Chicken With Sweet Potato Wedges

**Ingredients:**

- 2 sweet potatoes, cut into wedges
- 1 tbsp olive oil
- 1 tsp smoked paprika
- 4 boneless, skinless chicken breasts
- Salt and pepper

**Directions:**

1. Preheat grill to mediumhigh heat.
2. Brush chicken breasts with olive oil and season with smoked paprika, salt, and pepper.
3. Grill chicken for 45 minutes per side or until cooked through.
4. Toss sweet potato wedges with olive oil, salt, and pepper.

5. Grill sweet potato wedges for 34 minutes per side or until tender.
6. Serve grilled chicken with sweet potato wedges.

## Grilled Chicken Salad

**Ingredients:**

- 1 small red bell pepper
- 1 small yellow bell pepper
- 1/4 cup olive oil
- Salt and pepper
- 2 boneless, skinless chicken breasts
- 1 head of lettuce
- 1 small red onion

**Directions:**

1. Preheat a grill to mediumhigh heat.
2. Season chicken with salt and pepper and grill until cooked through, about 57 minutes per side.

3. Let chicken rest for 5 minutes and then slice into thin strips.
4. In a large bowl, combine lettuce, onion, and bell peppers.
5. Drizzle olive oil over the salad and toss to combine.
6. Add sliced chicken to the top of the salad and serve.

# Papayalime Juice

## Ingredients:

- 200g of Papaya
- 1 lime (juiced)
- 100ml of water

## Directions:

1. Remove the papaya's peel and seeds by cutting it in half.
2. Put the papaya in a juicer after chopping it into tiny pieces.
3. One lime's juice should be squeezed into the juicer.
4. Add 100ml of water.
5. The components should be well juiced.
6. Serve right away.

# Cranberryapple Juice

**Ingredients:**

- 200g of fresh cranberries
- 200g of apples
- 120ml of water

**Directions:**

1. Wash the apples and cranberries.
2. Apples should be peeled and cut into tiny pieces.
3. Juice the cranberries, apples, and water in a juicer until smooth.
4. Through a sieve with fine mesh, pass the mixture.
5. Enjoy the juice after serving.

## Lemonblueberry Juice

**Ingredients:**

- 2 tablespoons of honey
- 480ml of cold water
- Ice cubes for serving
- 400g of fresh blueberries
- 120ml of lemons juices

**Directions:**

1. Wash the blueberries thoroughly and remove any stems or leaves.
2. In a juicer, add the blueberries, lemon juice, honey, and water.
3. Juice on high speed until all the Ingredients: are well amalgamate.

4. Taste the mixture and adjust the sweetness with more honey, if desired.
5. Use a finemesh sieve to strain the juice and remove any pulp.
6. Transfer the juice to a pitcher or individual serving glasses.
7. Add ice cubes to each glass and serve right away.

**Acaiblueberry Smoothie Bowl**

**Ingredients:**

- 2 Tbsp fresh blueberries
- 1 Tbsp chopped toasted pecans
- ½ tsp chia seeds
- 3 ½ oz frozen unsweetened pure acai fruit puree
- ½ cup frozen mixed berries
- 10 Tbsp plain whole milk yogurt, divided
- ¼ cup unsweetened vanilla almond milk
- 2 tsp honey

**Directions:**

1. In a blender, combine acai fruit puree, frozen berries, 8 tablespoons of the yogurt, the

almond milk, and honey. Cover and blend until smooth.

2. Pour smoothie into a bowl. Top with remaining 2 tablespoons yogurt, the fresh blueberries, pecans, and chia seeds.

## Egginahole With Spinach & Bacon

**Ingredients:**

- 3 large cloves garlic, minced
- 1 pound spinach (about 16 cups), tough stems removed
- 1 teaspoon redwine vinegar
- ½ teaspoon ground pepper, divided
- ¼ teaspoon salt
- 3 slices centercut bacon
- 1 tablespoon extravirgin olive oil, plus more if needed
- 4 large slices countrystyle wholewheat bread (3/41 inch thick)
- 4 large eggs

**Directions:**

1. Preheat oven to 425 degrees F. Coat a large baking sheet with cooking spray.
2. Cook bacon in a large castiron skillet over medium heat until crisp, 7 to 9 minutes. Drain on paper towels.
3. Pour the bacon fat into a small heatproof bowl. If necessary, add oil to make 2 tablespoons.
4. Meanwhile, heat 1 tablespoon oil in a large saucepan over medium heat. Add garlic and cook, stirring, about 30 seconds.
5. Add spinach by the handful and cook, stirring, until wilted, about 5 minutes.
6. Transfer 47
7. to a colander; press out excess liquid. Return the spinach to the pan and season with vinegar, ¼ teaspoon pepper and salt.
8. Cut a 3 ½inch hole in the middle of each slice of bread. (Save the rounds for another use, if

desired.) Heat 1 tablespoon of the reserved bacon fat in the skillet over mediumhigh heat. Cook 2 slices of bread, pressing with a spatula, until lightly browned, 1 to 3 minutes per side.

9. Transfer to the prepared baking sheet. Repeat with the remaining fat and bread. Fill each hole with spinach. Make a deep well in the spinach and break an egg into each well.

10. Bake, rotating the baking sheet 180 degrees about halfway through, 10 to 14 minutes for softset yolks. Serve sprinkled with crumbled bacon and the remaining ¼ teaspoon pepper.

## Parmesan Cloud Eggs

**Ingredients:**

- 1 scallion, finely chopped
- Ground pepper to taste
- 4 large eggs, yolks and whites separated
- Pinch of salt
- ¼ cup finely grated Parmesan cheese

**Directions:**

1. Preheat oven to 450 degrees F. Line a large baking sheet with parchment paper. Lightly coat with cooking spray.
2. Separate egg whites from the yolks, placing each yolk in an individual small bowl.

3. Beat all of the egg whites and salt in a mixing bowl with an electric mixer on high speed until stiff.
4. Gently fold Parmesan and scallions into the beaten whites with a rubber spatula.
5. Make 4 mounds (about ¾ cup each) of eggcheese mixture on the prepared baking sheet. Make a well in the middle of each mound with the back of a spoon.
6. Bake the egg whites until starting to lightly brown, about 3 minutes.
7. Remove from oven. If the well has filled in during baking, use the spoon to recreate it.
8. Gently slip a yolk into each well. Bake until the yolks are cooked but still runny, 3 to 5 minutes more. Sprinkle with pepper. Serve immediately.

**Raised Pork Pie**

**Ingredients:**

**For the filling**

- 2 large pinches ground nutmeg
- 1 tbsp fresh chopped sage
- 1 tsp fresh chopped thyme
- ½ tsp salt
- 1 tsp ground white pepper
- 800g pork shoulder, minced or finely chopped
- 400g pork belly, half minced and half chopped
- 250g smoked bacon, cubed
- ½ tsp ground mace

**For the pastry**

- 575g plain flour

- 200g lard

- 220ml water

**To finish**

- 1 egg, beaten

- 6 gelatine leaves

- 300ml chicken stock

**Directions:**

1. Heat the oven to 180C/160C fan/gas 4. In a large bowl mix together all the **Ingredients:**for the filling.
2. To make the pastry, put the flour in a large bowl, then put the lard and water into a small pan and heat gently until the lard melts.
3. Bring just to the boil and then stir into the flour using a wooden spoon. When the

mixture is cool enough to handle, (it should still feel very warm) knead well until smooth.
4. Cut off 1/4 of the dough, wrap in cling film and reserve for the lid.
5. Roll out the remaining dough to a circle and then place in the base of a nonstick 20cm springform cake tin.
6. Working quickly while the dough is warm and pliable, press the dough evenly over the base and up the sides of the tin.
7. Make sure there are no holes. Fill with the meat mixture and pack down well. Roll out the dough for the lid.
8. Place on top of the pie. Pinch all around the edge to seal the pie. Make a hole for steam in the centre, using the handle of a wooden spoon.
9. Cook in the oven for 30 mins then reduce the heat to 160C/140C fan/gas 3 and cook for 90 minutes. Brush the top with beaten egg and

return to the oven for a further 20 mins. Leave until cold.

10. Soak the gelatine in cold water for about 5 mins, then remove and squeeze out the excess water.
11. Heat the stock until almost boiling. Remove from the heat and stir in the gelatine. Leave to cool to room temperature.
12. Use a small funnel to pour the stock into the pie through the hole in the top. Pour in a little at a time allowing a few seconds before each addition. Place in the fridge to set overnight.
13. Watch our pork pie video for techniques and tips.

## Ginger Chicken & Green Bean Noodles

**Ingredients:**

- 2 garlic cloves, sliced

- 1 ball stem ginger, finely sliced, plus 1 tsp syrup from the jar

- 1 tsp cornflour, mixed with 1 tbsp water

- 1 tsp dark soy sauce, plus extra to serve (optional)

- 2 tsp rice vinegar

- ½ tbsp vegetable oil

- 2 skinless chicken breasts, sliced

- 200g green beans, trimmed and halved crosswise

- thumbsized piece of ginger, peeled and cut into matchsticks
- 200g cooked egg noodles

**Directions:**

1. Heat the oil in a wok over a high heat and stirfry the chicken for 5 mins. Add the green beans and stirfry for 45 mins more until the green beans are just tender, and the chicken is just cooked through.
2. Stir in the fresh ginger and garlic, and stirfry for 2 mins, then add the stem ginger and syrup, the cornflour mix, soy sauce and vinegar.
3. Stirfry for 1 min, then toss in the noodles. Cook until everything is hot and the sauce coats the noodles. Drizzle with more soy, if you like, and serve.

# Teriyaki Salmon With Grilled Zucchini

**Ingredients:**

- 2 (6oz.) fillets of salmon
- 5 tbsp. Teriyaki sauce, lowsodium
- 2 zucchini, sliced thin
- 4 chopped scallions
- Sesame seeds
- Coconut oil

**Directions:**

1. Marinade the salmon with the teriyaki sauce for 25 minutes in a ziptop bag.
2. Toast the sesame seeds in a large skillet on medium heat, the set the sesame seeds aside.

3. Add the salmon (without the marinade) to a hot skillet and cook on medium heat for around 5 minutes each side.
4. Remove salmon from heat and keep it warm while adding the scallions, zucchini and 1 tbsp. of oil to the skillet and sauté until browned.
5. Stir in 2 tbsp. of teriyaki sauce, and sprinkle over sesame seeds.
6. Serve with the salmon.

## Savory Brown Rice With Vegetables

**Ingredients:**

- 10 chopped grape tomatoes
- 1 tablespoon chopped parsley
- 1/2 tablespoon chopped basil
- 2 oz Kalamata black olives
- Salt and freshly milled black pepper
- 1 large onion chopped
- 1 clove of garlic crushed
- 2 tablespoons coconut oil
- 4 oz sliced mushrooms
- 3 cups of cooked brown rice

**Directions:**

1. Gently sweat the onion and garlic in the coconut oil
2. When it is soft, add the mushrooms and cook for about 5 minutes
3. Add the chopped tomatoes, herbs, seasoning and olives
4. Finally stir in the rice and keep turning until the mixture has heated through.

## Shrimp And Brown Rice Risotto

**Ingredients:**

- 3 cups of lowsodium vegetable stock
- Pinch of saffron
- ½ cup of red wine vinegar
- 1 cup mushrooms
- 1 tbsp. chopped parsley
- 2 oz. almond butter
- 2 tablespoons extra virgin olive oil
- 2 cups short grain brown rice (uncooked)
- 1 chopped onion
- 1 clove chopped garlic
- 3 cups of deveined cooked shrimp

**Directions:**

1. In a large pan melt the almond butter and oil over a low heat
2. Stir in the rice and cook gently for about 10 minutes
3. Add the onion and garlic and cook for 5 minutes
4. Add half the vegetable stock and cook gently until the stock is absorbed
5. Mix the saffron, wine vinegar and remaining stock together and add to the rice with the mushrooms and shrimp
6. Cover and allow it to cook gently until all the liquid is absorbed  Add the parsley and serve

# Blueberry Basil Weight Loss Smoothie

**Ingredients:**

- 1/4 cup 2% plain Greek Yogurt
- 1 Tablespoon lemon juice
- 1 Tablespoon ground flaxseed
- 1 Tablespoon almond butter
- 2 cups frozen blueberries
- 1 frozen banana
- 1/21 cup unsweetened vanilla almond milk
- 1/4 cup 56 leaves fresh basil

**Directions:**

1. Blend: Place all Ingredients: in a highpowered blender and blend until smooth.

2. Start with 1/2 cup of almond milk and add more if needed to reach the desired consistency.
3. Serve: Pour into a glass and enjoy!

## Cabbage Fatburning Soup

**Ingredients:**

- 2 green bell peppers, diced
- 1 large head cabbage, chopped
- 1 (15 ounce) can cut green beans, drained
- 2 quarts tomato juice
- 2 (16 ounce) cans whole peeled tomatoes, with liquid
- 1 (14 ounce) can beef broth
- cold water, to cover
- 10 stalks celery, chopped
- 5 carrots, chopped
- 3 onions, chopped

- 1 (1 ounce) envelope dry onion soup mix

**Directions:**

1. Place celery, carrots, onions, cabbage, bell peppers, and green beans in a large soup pot.
2. Add tomato juice, tomatoes, beef broth, and enough water to cover vegetables; add onion soup mix and stir to combine.
3. Bring to a boil over medium heat; reduce heat to low and simmer until vegetables are tender, about 25 minutes.

## Drink With Mango & Basil

**INGREDIENTS:**

- 1 litre plain drinking water
- 1/2 medium sized ripe mango cut in cubes
- 56 basil leaves

**DIRECTIONS:**

1. In a large glass jar add in plain water, peeled and cubed pieces of mango along with washed and cleaned basil leaves.
2. Stir in all the additions into the water so that they don't settle at the bottom of the jar.
3. Cover the jar with a lid and allow this water to be infused with all the goodness of the basil leaves and mangoes. Allow to steep at least for 6 hours, but overnight is preferred. You may refrigerate the jar of water as well.

4. The next morning pour out the water into a drinking glass, and drink instead of plain water or high calorie sodas.
5. You can use the same ingredients by changing the water two times, after which, discard the mangoes and basil leaves and make a fresh batch.

## Chicken Piccata

**Ingredients:**

- 4 Tbsp olive oil
- 2 freshly squeezed lemon juice
- 2 Tbsp chopped fresh parsley
- 2 tsp capers, minced
- 12 ounces boneless, skinless chicken tenders
- 2 Tbsp flour
- Freshly ground black pepper

**Directions:**

1. LAY the tenders on a work surface. With a smooth scaloppine pounder or a rolling pin covered in plastic wrap, flatten to 1/4"

thickness. Dredge the cutlets lightly in the flour.

2. HEAT a large skillet over mediumhigh heat. Add the oil to the skillet and heat until sizzling. Place the chicken in the skillet. Cook for 2 minutes per side or until lightly browned and cooked through.

3. ADD the lemon juice, parsley, and capers. Bring the mixture to a boil. Reduce the heat and simmer for 2 minutes to allow the flavors to blend. Season to taste with the pepper. Serve the chicken with the pan juices.

## Slow Cooker African Chicken Stew

**Ingredients:**

- 1 sweet potato, peeled and cubed
- 1 can (14½ ounces) reducedsodium chicken broth
- 1/2 cup chunky natural unsalted peanut butter
- 2 Tbsp tomato paste
- 1/4 tsp salt
- 1/4 tsp freshly ground black pepper
- 1 Tbsp peanut oil
- 12 ounces boneless, skinless chicken thighs, trimmed and cut into 24 pieces
- 1 onion, chopped

- 3 cloves garlic, minced

- 1 jalapeno chile pepper, seeded and chopped

- 1 carrot, thickly sliced

**Directions:**

1. HEAT the oil in a large nonstick skillet over mediumhigh heat.
2. Add the chicken and cook, stirring occasionally, for 3 to 4 minutes or until lightly browned.
3. Transfer to a 4quart slow cooker. Return the skillet to the heat and add the onion, garlic, chile pepper, and carrot.
4. Cook for 1 minute, then transfer to the slow cooker. Stir in the sweet potato, broth, peanut butter, and tomato paste.
5. COOK on high for 3 to 4 hours or low for 5 to 6 hours or until the chicken and vegetables are

very tender. Season with salt and black pepper.

## Greek Yogurt With Chia Seeds

**Ingredients:**

- 2 cups of Greek yogurt
- 2 tablespoons of chia seeds
- 1/4 cup of honey
- 1/4 cup of fresh or frozen berries (optional)

**Directions:**

1. In a medium bowl, combine the Greek yogurt and chia seeds. Stir to combine.
2. Add honey and mix until evenly distributed.
3. If desired, add the fresh or frozen berries and mix until evenly distributed.
4. Refrigerate the yogurt mixture for at least 1 hour before serving.

5. Serve cold, topped with additional honey and/or fresh or frozen berries if desired. Enjoy!

## Hummus And Veggies

**Ingredients:**

- 2 tablespoons tahini
- 2 tablespoons olive oil
- 3 tablespoons lemon juice
- Salt and pepper to taste
- 1/4 teaspoon cumin
- 1/4 teaspoon paprika
- 1 can chickpeas, drained and rinsed
- 2 cloves garlic
- Assortment of fresh or cooked vegetables of your choice

**Directions:**

1. In a blender or food processor, combine the chickpeas, garlic, tahini, olive oil, lemon juice, salt, pepper, cumin, and paprika. Blend until smooth.
2. Transfer the hummus to a bowl and serve with the vegetables of your choice. Enjoy!

**Baked Sweet Potato With Black Beans And Salad**

**Ingredients:**

- 2 cups mixed greens
- 1/4 cup diced red onion
- 1/4 cup diced cherry tomatoes
- 2 Tablespoons balsamic vinegar
- 2 Tablespoons olive oil
- 2 large sweet potatoes
- 1 can of black beans that have been washed and drained
- 2 Tablespoons olive oil
- 1 teaspoon cumin
- 1 teaspoon chili powder

- Salt and pepper to taste

**Directions:**

1. Preheat oven to 400°F.
2. Place sweet potatoes on a baking sheet and bake for 3035
3. minutes, until tender.
4. Put a skillet on average heat and add 2 Tablespoons of olive oil Add the black beans and season with cumin, chili powder, salt, and pepper. Cook for 57 minutes, stirring occasionally.
5. In a large bowl, combine the mixed greens, red onion, and cherry tomatoes.
6. Mix the olive oil and balsamic vinegar in a small basin.
7. Once the sweet potatoes are done baking, top them with the black beans.
8. Drizzle the balsamic vinaigrette over the salad and toss to combine.

9. Serve the salad alongside the sweet potatoes and enjoy!

## Grilled Chicken With Zucchini Noodles

**Ingredients:**

- 2 cloves garlic, minced
- 1 teaspoon dried Italian seasoning
- 2 boneless, skinless chicken breasts
- Two medium zucchini, spiralized or cut into noodles 2 tablespoons olive oil
- Salt and pepper to taste
- Fresh basil, chopped (optional)

**Directions:**

1. Preheat the grill to low heat.
2. Season the chicken breasts with pepper, salt, and dried Italian seasoning.
3. Grill the chicken for about 67 minutes per side or until cooked through.

4. While the chicken is grilling, heat olive oil in a large skillet over medium heat.
5. Add minced garlic to the skillet and cook for about 1
6. minute until fragrant.
7. Add the zucchini noodles to the skillet and sauté for 23 minutes until they are tendercrisp.
8. Season with salt and pepper.
9. Slice the grilled chicken and serve it on top of the zucchini noodles.
10. Garnish with fresh basil if desired.

**Cauliflower Crust Pizza**

**Ingredients:**

- 1/4 teaspoon garlic powder

- 1 large egg, beaten

- Pizza sauce

- Assorted pizza toppings (e.g., sliced bell peppers, mushrooms, olives)

- 1 small head of cauliflower, grated or riced 1/2 cup shredded mozzarella cheese

- 1/4 cup grated Parmesan cheese

- 1 teaspoon dried Italian seasoning

- Shredded mozzarella cheese for topping

**Directions:**

1. Preheat the oven to 425°F (220°C) and using parchment paper line a baking sheet.
2. Place the grated or riced cauliflower in a microwavesafe bowl and microwave for close to 5 minutes.
3. Allow the cauliflower to cool slightly and then move it to a clean kitchen towel or cheesecloth.
4. Squeeze out as much liquid as possible out from the cauliflower.
5. In a mixing bowl, combine the cauliflower, shredded mozzarella cheese, grated Parmesan cheese, dried Italian seasoning, garlic powder, and beaten egg.
6. Mix everything together until well combined.
7. Move the cauliflower mixture onto the prepared baking sheet and shape it into a round pizza crust.

8. Bake in the preheated oven for close to 1520 minutes until the crust is golden brown and crispy.
9. Remove from the oven and spread pizza sauce over the crust.
10. Add your favorite pizza toppings and sprinkle shredded mozzarella cheese on top.
11. Return the pizza back to the oven and bake for another 1012 minutes until the cheese is melted and a bit bubbly.
12. Slice and serve the cauliflower crust pizza for a flavorful and lowcarb dinner.

# Roasted Chickpeas

**Ingredients:**

- 1 teaspoon paprika
- 1 teaspoon garlic powder
- 1 can chickpeas, drained and rinsed
- 12 tablespoons olive oil
- Salt and pepper, to taste

**Directions:**

1. Preheat your oven to 400°F (200°C).
2. Drain and rinse the chickpeas and pat them dry with a paper towel.
3. In a bowl, mix together the chickpeas, olive oil, paprika, garlic powder, salt, and pepper until the chickpeas are evenly coated.

4. Spread the chickpeas out on a baking sheet lined with parchment paper.
5. Roast the chickpeas in the oven for 2025 minutes, or until they are golden brown and crispy.
6. Let the chickpeas cool for a few minutes before serving.

## Creamy Green Smoothie

**Ingredients:**

- 1/2 cup plain Greek yogurt
- 1 tablespoon honey
- 1/2 teaspoon vanilla extract
- 1 cup unsweetened almond milk
- 1 cup spinach
- 1/2 cup kale
- 1/2 medium avocado
- 1 medium banana
- 1/2 cup ice

**Directions:**

1. Rinse the spinach and kale leaves and remove the stems.
2. Peel and chop the avocado and banana.
3. Add the spinach, kale, avocado, banana, Greek yogurt, honey, and vanilla extract to a blender.
4. Add the almond milk and ice to the blender.
5. Blend until smooth.
6. Pour the smoothie into two glasses and enjoy!

## Pineapple And Kale Smoothie

**Ingredients:**

- 1/2 cup plain Greek yogurt
- 1 tablespoon chia seeds
- 1 cup unsweetened almond milk
- 1/2 cup ice
- 2 cups kale leaves, washed and chopped
- 1 cup chopped fresh pineapple
- 1/2 medium banana

**Directions:**

1. Rinse the kale leaves and remove the stems.
2. Peel and chop the pineapple and banana.

3. Add the kale, pineapple, banana, Greek yogurt, chia seeds, and almond milk to a blender.
4. Add the ice to the blender.
5. Blend until smooth.
6. Pour the smoothie into two glasses and enjoy!

## Mango And Celery Smoothie

**Ingredients:**

- ½ cup mango chunks
- 1 cup coconut water
- 1 cup kale leaves, chopped
- ½ cup fresh parsley
- 1 medium stalk of celery

**Directions:**

1. Clean and prepare the greens.
2. Cut the celery stalk into 1inch pieces to simplify mixing.
3. In a blender, combine all Ingredients: and mix until smooth.
4. Strain into a glass and serve.

## Fruity Green Smoothie

**Ingredients:**

- 1 ripe banana, sliced
- 1 cup cubed pears
- 1 cup purified water
- ½ cup kale leaves, chopped
- ½ cup fresh baby spinach leaves
- ½ cup fresh berries (raspberry or strawberry)

**Directions:**

1. Combine the water, kale, and spinach in a blender. Blend until smooth.
2. Add the other Ingredients: and whisk until smooth.
3. Pour into a glass and serve right away.

www.ingramcontent.com/pod-product-compliance
Lightning Source LLC
LaVergne TN
LVHW010222070526
838199LV00062B/4691